RESTO

of

HOLY GIVING

RELEASING THE TRUE
1,000 FOLD BLESSING

DOMINIQUAE
BIERMAN

Unless otherwise identified, Scripture quotations are from: The King James Version or New American Standard Bible. Used by permission. All rights reserved.

Published by Zion's Gospel Press

52 Tuscan Way, Ste 202-412
St. Augustine, FL, 32092
shalom@zionsgospel.com

Paperback ISBN: 978-1-953502-47-6
E-Book ISBN: 978-1-953502-48-3

On occasion words such as Jesus, Christ, Lord and God have been changed by the author, back to their original Hebrew renderings, Yeshua, Messiah, Yahveh, and Elohim.

Bold or italicized emphasis or underlining within quotations is the author's own.

Printed in the United States of America

First Printing September 2012, Second Printing April 2013, Third Printing June 2021

The wicked earns deceptive wages, but he who sows righteousness gets a true reward.

—Proverbs 11:18

CONTENTS

Chapter 1

Restoring Righteous Giving

For where your treasure is,
there your heart will be also.
—Matthew 6:21

W hen we return to the Jewish roots of the faith
and the apostolic Hebrew foundations, we must
also restore holy giving. Replacement theology has affected
the Body of Yeshua in many areas and especially in the area of
giving. Most people do not know how to give, who to give to
and when to give; thus, they never come out of spiritual and/
or financial drought.

Holy giving is a matter of the heart; therefore, it comes
from the Heart of Elohim (God) Himself! He showed us the
way in the arena of giving by giving us the highest He could
give, His only begotten Son, His Blood on the altar so that you

and I can be rescued from sin and Satan! *Yeshua was Elohim's first fruits offering and He gave Him to us.*

For God so loved the world; that He gave His only begotten Son, that whoever believes in Him shall not perish, but have eternal life.

—John 3:16

When we have Yeshua's character, then we are givers by nature.

In everything I showed you that by working hard in this manner you must help the weak and remember the words of the LORD Yeshua, that He Himself said, 'It is more blessed to give than to receive.

—Acts 20:35

Sowing Right

The Apostle Shaul-Paul tells us that giving financially is like "sowing," and he uses farming terms to describe the way that giving affects us.

Now this I say, he who sows sparingly will also reap sparingly, and he who sows bountifully will also reap bountifully.

—2 Corinthians 9:6

Any farmer will tell you that there is no way to reap if we do not sow and that the abundance of the crop depends on the quality and quantity of the seed sown.

The quality of the seed is determined by the attitude of the giver—if it is given in obedience to Yah's (God's) Commandments (see prescribed giving and sacrificial giving) and with a cheerful, generous heart or not.

Each one must do just as he has purposed in his heart, not grudgingly or under compulsion, for God loves a cheerful giver.

—2 Corinthians 9:7

The quantity of the seed is also important, and it depends on the means of everyone. The widow that gave one mite (the smallest coin) gave more than the rich people that put thousands into the treasury, for her mite was *all* she had to give.

It provoked Yeshua's attention!

And He sat down opposite the treasury, and began observing how the people were putting money into the treasury; and many rich people were putting in large sums. A poor widow came and put in two small copper coins, which amount to a cent. Calling His disciples to Him, He said to them, "Truly I say to you, this poor widow put in more than all the contributors to the treasury; for they all put in out of their surplus, but she, out of her poverty, put in all she owned, all she had to live on.

—Mark 12:41-44

We do not know what happened with that widow, but most probably, she got miraculously blessed, for she had sowed in quality and quantity bountifully. If she would have eaten her seed instead of sowing the little she had, she would have stayed poor forever! Any farmer will tell you that you should not eat your seed. When people tell me "I cannot tithe," "I cannot give for I am very poor," I know that person is in terrible deception of unbelief, and he/she has been eating their seed. The Word of God says that He gives seed to the sower! In other words, if you are not a sower, you will have no seed because you will eat it up! And if you are not a sower, do not expect to be a reaper.

Now He who supplies seed to the sower and bread for food will supply and multiply your seed for sowing and increase the harvest of your righteousness.

—2 Corinthians 9:10

He can only multiply the seed that is *sown*, not the seed that you have eaten. If you become a sower, YHVH will give you seed, but be careful not to eat it but to sow it.

No Leftovers, Please

Wrong giving or lack of prescribed giving such as tithes, first fruits and feast offerings can incur a terrible curse and is the number one issue of repentance before revival can come.

But when you present the blind for sacrifice, is it not evil? And when you present the lame and sick, is it not evil? Why not offer it to your governor? Would he be pleased with you? Or would he receive you kindly?" says the LORD of hosts. "But now will you not entreat God's favor, that He may be gracious to us? With such an offering on your part, will He receive any of you kindly?" says the LORD of hosts.

—Malachi 1:8,9

It is clear from this passage that the right kind of giving can incur Elohim-God's favor, and the wrong kind of giving incur His displeasure and disfavor.

Most people give Yah (God) only what they have left over and that always will incur His displeasure as it is terribly dishonoring to give Him "leftovers!" The leftovers are to be given to the poor, not to the Almighty. It is obvious that Elohim does not need any money, but when you give to His priests/ministers of the gospel and servants, it is to Him that you are giving. Here is an important principle:

Do not ever give leftovers to your bishops, pastors, mentors, teachers, rabbis, prophets, apostles or to anyone that is blessing you spiritually as it is dishonoring. They do not need your "charity"; they are not beggars. They carry the highest and most important positions under Heaven.

Later on, in this letter, you will see what the prescribed offerings for God's ministers are.

The one who is taught the Word is to share all good things with the one who teaches him. Do not be deceived, God is not mocked; for whatever a man sows, this he will also reap. For the one who sows to his own flesh will from the flesh reap corruption, but the one who sows to the Spirit will from the Spirit reap eternal life.
—Galatians 6:6,7

Those that do not bless their pastors and teachers financially are mocking God Himself, and instead of reaping spiritual blessings, they will reap corruption. This is a very serious warning!

And here is another most important principle: If you take care of those who teach the Word to you, YHVH will take care of you. If your minister is poor, you will be poor spiritually and eventually also financially. If your bishop, pastor, teacher, mentor is well-taken care of financially, so will Yah (God) do to you in both the financial and the spiritual arena, for a disciple is never greater than his master.

A disciple is not above his teacher, nor a slave above his master.
—Matthew 10:24

So if your bishop, pastor, teacher, mentor is blessed financially, rejoice! Now you can be blessed, too, especially if you are a sower. It is time to break out of the false teachings that promote poverty among God's ministers. It is true that sometimes we have a lot and sometimes a little, but there is no Scripture supporting the theology that God's servants need to be poor. As a matter of fact, we see exactly the opposite. Even our fathers, Abraham, Isaac and Jacob, were so rich that they were a threat to the local kings! Paul the Apostle himself, who suffered much hardship, was carrying very often large sums of money and many offerings given to him for his own needs, for ministry and for distribution.

[For] we are on our guard, intending that no one should find anything for which to blame us in regard to our administration of this large contribution.
—2 Corinthians 8:20

6

Categories of Giving

1. Prescribed Giving
2. Freewill Giving
3. Sacrificial Giving
4. Restitution Giving

Prescribed Giving

The Torah is very explicit about prescribed giving. It tells us *who* to give, *how much* to give and *when* to give.

WHO, HOW MUCH, & WHEN?

- Priests and Levites – Tithes, First Fruits, Offerings, Feast Offerings
- Widows, Orphans, Strangers, Poor – Alms, Corners of the Field and Third Year Tithe
- Ourselves and our families – Feast Tithes

PRIESTS & LEVITES

The Torah is clear about giving to those who officiate in the work of the Tabernacle. Those are likened unto the Five-Fold Ministries today, and they are the modern-day priests and Levites. Just imagine your life with no pastors, teachers, evangelists and so forth. Some of us got saved because of an evangelist, some of us got baptized in the Holy Spirit because an apostle or prophet ministered to us. Some of us got delivered from evil spirits when a bishop or a pastor prayed for us and so many more examples of spiritual and practical blessings into our lives happened because God's ministers were in their position!

And He gave some as apostles, and some as prophets, and some as evangelists, and some as pastors and teachers, for the equipping of the saints for the work of service, to the building up of the body of Messiah.

—Ephesians 4:11, 12

In order to keep these servants, ministers, "body builders" in shape and in their position, the Almighty established a system of giving, which I will call Holy Giving. In the world, people also give bountifully to their "gurus": favorite football team, singers, psychic readers and the like, which is unholy giving. They give hefty sums to those that "build them up." How is it that in the Body of Yeshua, it is not clearly understood that Holy Giving to God's servants is mandatory if they are to perform their duties? Paul warns us not to be deceived about this issue, as it will cause mockery to the Living God.

The one who is taught the Word is to share all good things with the one who teaches him. Do not be deceived, God is not mocked; for whatever a man sows, this he will also reap.

—Galatians 6:6

FIRST FRUITS

The first of all the first fruits of every kind and every contribution of every kind, from all your contributions, shall be for the priests;

you shall also give to the priest the first of your dough to cause a blessing to rest on your house.

—Ezekiel 44:30

This is the first offering mentioned in the Holy Scriptures when Abel offered it to YHVH.

So it came about in the course of time that Cain brought an offering to YHVH of the fruit of the ground. Abel, on his part also brought of the firstlings *of his flock and of their fat portions. And the* Lord *had regard for Abel and for his offering.*

—Genesis 4:3,4

Notice that YHVH received with favor the offering of Abel as it was a first fruit offering, and Cain's He did not receive because it was "an offering" or whatever Cain wanted and not what is prescribed.

The first fruits offering is an offering of *honor*. We honor YHVH with it!

Honor YHVH from your wealth and from the first of all your produce; So your barns will be filled with plenty and your vats will overflow with new wine.

—Proverbs 3:9,10

The first fruits offering has to be given to the priest so he can bless you!

In other words, when we give the first fruits to Elohim's ministers that are assigned to bless us, it is Elohim Himself that we are honoring in that minister. The promise is dual:

- Your barns (bank accounts) will be filled with *plenty*
- Your vats (spiritual life) will be filled with *new wine* (newness in the spirit and revival)
- How do you calculate first fruits in a non-agricultural society?

Monthly Firstfruits

Whether you are a business person or receive a salary: divide your income per 26 moon days (excluding Shabbat). The best time to give it is during the Rosh Chodesh (New Moon; see Jewish calendar or site the moon) or at the start of every month.

Random First Fruits

Those are special blessings that occur once in a while. For example, when I received the *first* check in my life with royalties for one of my songs, it was a first fruit, so I gave it all to Yah (God). When you start a new job, your *first* paycheck or a new business, your *first* revenue, etc. When I print a new book that I have never printed before, normally the first box or the first book I give away to ministers as first fruits. As you are sensitive to the Holy Spirit, Yah will show you what these special occasions are.

Sacrificial First Fruits

This is when Elohim requires the best or all that you have. This particular first fruit is the *most* powerful kind of giving, for it provokes a "cosmic" response from Heaven that can change the course of history. It is called *a potent seed*. It engages the Almighty in such a way that the benefits of these particular first fruits can be reaped for many generations to come and forever! Isaac was the first fruit of Abraham from Sarah, his wife. Elohim required this extravagant first fruit, and when Abraham speedily obeyed him, it engaged the Almighty in releasing *all* His blessing unto Abraham and *all* his generations and to send us Elohim's own Son to save us all. Think about it the next time that He requires from you the best or all that you have!

By Myself I have sworn, declares YHVH, because you have done this thing and have not withheld your son, your only son, indeed I will greatly bless you, and I will greatly multiply your seed as the stars of the heavens and as the sand which is on the seashore; and your seed shall possess the gate of their enemies. In your seed all the nations of the earth shall be blessed, because you have obeyed My voice.

—Genesis 22:16-18

Chapter 2

Prescribed Giving
to Priests & Ministers

And, behold, I have given the Levites all the
tithes in Israel for an inheritance in return for
their service which they serve, the service of the
Tent of Meeting.
—Numbers 18:21

L et us remember that there are four categories of giving: Prescribed giving, Freewill giving, Sacrificial giving and Restitution giving.

The Tithes Are Holy to YHVH

And all the tithe of the land, whether of the seed of the land or of
the fruit of the tree, is the LORD's; it is holy to YHVH. And if a

man wants to redeem any of his tithe, he shall add a fifth to it. And all the tithe of the herd or of the flock, whatever passes under the herdsman's staff [by means of which each tenth animal as it passes through a small door is selected and marked], the tenth shall be holy to YHVH.

—Leviticus 27:30-32

Holy is 'Kadosh' in Hebrew, which means set apart, not for common use. They are so holy that if you use them, you must pay it back with a 20% increase (a fifth).

There are *three* categories of tithes:

1. The First Tithe – Belongs in its entirety to the Levites
2. The Third Year Tithe – It is shared between the Levites, the widow, the orphan and the stranger
3. The Feast Tithe – It is shared between you, your family and servants and the officiating Levites

Tithes For the Levites – the First Tithe

But the tithes of the Israelites, which they present as an offering to the LORD, I have given to the Levites to inherit; therefore I have said to them, Among the Israelites they shall have no inheritance. [They have homes and cities and pasturage to use but not to possess as their personal inheritance.]

—*Numbers 18:24*

The Torah talks about three kinds of tithes, and the Levites receive a portion from all of them. However, theirs is the *first tithe*!

And, behold, I have given the Levites all the tithes in Israel for an inheritance in return for their service which they serve, the service of the Tent of Meeting.

—Numbers 18:21

These tithes are so important that the Word calls it "Holy Tithes," and they are to be shared between the Levites (Torah, Word teachers, pastors, bishops) and the singers (the worship team) and even others in full-time ministry. When these tithes are not distributed to these servants of Yah, then they are in danger of forsaking their post due to lack of income, and rightly so.

I also discovered that the portions of the Levites had not been given them, so that the Levites and the singers who performed the service had gone away, each to his own field.

—Nehemiah 13:10

During the days of Nehemiah, there was a great revival in Judah, and the key for this revival was repentance for breaking Yah's (God's) commandments and the reinstitution of a Holy and sanctified Priesthood.

On that day men were also appointed over the chambers for the stores, the contributions, the first fruits and the tithes, to gather into them from the fields of the cities the portions required by the law for the priests and Levites; for Judah rejoiced over the priests and Levites who served.

—Nehemiah 12:44

The mark of this revival, like *all* revivals, was *joyful giving* so that the priests and the Levites could minister freely without any financial concerns. Today most of the Five Fold ministers and worship leaders are too concerned about "making a living" instead of concentrating on seeking Yah's presence and studying His Word! This is a pitiful state of affairs, and it is affecting the entire Body. The tithes just simply do not reach the ministers, and most of them are suffering financially. How do we want them to be ministering with joy if there is no food on the table for their children or money to buy new clothes and pay the mortgage and the electric bill? And what kind of testimony are the PKs (preacher's kids) getting about God? Truly if everyone in the Body of Yeshua would give their tithes to their ministers, there would be no lack, but the percentage of Christians/ Messianics that tithe is shameful. Most people say, "I cannot afford to tithe; the finances are 'shaky.'" I tell you, you cannot afford *not* to tithe, especially when the finances are shaky! If you do not honor God's servant, Elohim cannot honor you!

"From the days of your fathers you have turned aside from My statutes and have not kept them. Return to Me, and I will return to you," says the LORD of hosts. "But you say, 'How shall we return?'

—Malachi 3:7

This is one of the major issues that need *repentance* in the Body of Yeshua. The people in Malachi's time were suffering from financial shakings much like today, and they were asking YHVH what to do. He said, "*Teshuva* (Repent and Return)," and they asked, "what do we need to repent of?" His answer was: "You are robbing Me because you do not bring the prescribed tithes and offerings to the priests and Levites!"

"Will a man rob God? Yet you are robbing Me! But you say, 'How have we robbed You?' In tithes and offerings. You are cursed with a curse, for you are robbing Me, the whole nation of you! Bring the whole tithe into the storehouse, so that there may be food in My house, and test Me now in this," says the LORD of hosts, "if I will not open for you the windows of heaven and pour out for you a blessing until it overflows."

—Malachi 3:8-10

You see, the Tithes are prescribed seed, and if you eat your seed, especially in times of famine and financial shaking, all your hope for a harvest is gone. No seed, no harvest. It is only after one brings the whole tithe that the curse breaks and Elohim can keep His Word to rebuke the devourer and provide royally for you!

Then I will rebuke the devourer for you, so that it will not destroy the fruits of the ground; nor will your vine in the field cast its grapes," says the LORD of hosts. "All the nations will call you blessed, for you shall be a delightful land," says the LORD of hosts.

—Malachi 3:11-12

The Whole Tithe, What Is This?

This is 10% of all your income *before* you pay bills and debts! Most people give a 10% from the bottom after they pay their bills; therefore, they see no breakthrough.

MAKING RESTITUTION FOR ROBBING THE ALMIGHTY

The Word of God tells us that if we use the prescribed tithe and first fruits that belong to the priests and to the Levites, the ministers of the Word (bishops, pastors, teachers) and worship leaders, then we have to pay 20% more (a fifth) and make restitution to YHVH!

And if a man wants to redeem any of his tithe, he shall add a fifth to it.

—Leviticus 27:31

I wonder how many people owe tithes, first fruits and a 20% on top of it? That is a *big debt* and an urgent issue of repentance and restitution.

He shall make restitution for that which he has sinned against the holy thing, and shall add to it a fifth part of it and give it to the priest. The priest shall then make atonement for him with the ram of the guilt offering, and it will be forgiven him.

—Leviticus 5:16

Who is the priest or the Levite that has been teaching you the Word?

Have you blessed him/her with your first fruits and tithes? If you have defaulted, go ahead and ask their forgiveness and make installments to pay it in full plus 20% on top of it. That is true repentance and restitution!

I can imagine your flesh rising: How can I pay back all that? Well, why is it that in the world, we must pay back loans, mortgages and credit card debt and we make payments by installments until we are done? Isn't it much more important to be right with Elohim-God on this issue? We have been so religious that we have taken His instructions and ministers very lightly. No wonder the Body of Yeshua is in the shape it is!

At this point, your flesh may be screaming once again with the typical "Christian slogan": *I am not under the law; I am under grace!*

Does that mean that it is OK to break Yah's (God's) laws because we are under grace?

What happens if you break the laws of your country? Will you not go to jail? And if you say to the authorities: "Sorry, I did not know," will they dismiss the case, or will you have to make payments until your debt is finished?

What shall we say then? Is the Law sin? May it never be! On the contrary, I would not have come to know sin except through the Law; for I would not have known about coveting if the Law had not said, "you shall not covet. Therefore did that which is good become a cause of death for me? May it never be! Rather it was sin, in order that it might be shown to be sin by affecting my death through that which is good, so that through the commandment sin would become utterly sinful.

—Romans 7,13

So now, through the Torah (Law), you know that withholding your Holy first fruits and tithes from God's ministers that labor on your behalf is utterly sinful, and it requires a response of repentance and restitution!

What shall we say then? Are we to continue in sin so that grace may increase? May it never be! How shall we who died to sin still live in it?

—Romans 6:1-3

The Good News is that through the Blood of Yeshua, we can receive forgiveness of sin if we confess and forsake it.

If we confess our sins, He is faithful and righteous to forgive us our sins and to cleanse us from all unrighteousness.

—1 John 1:9

We must confess the sin of withholding first fruits and tithes to those that have mentored and taught us the Word and not only to YHVH.

In other words, go to those who pastor you and teach you and ask for forgiveness. It may be more than one minister; some are taught in a church, others through the internet or the writings of some teacher/preacher. You must decide in your mind and ask the Holy Spirit about those who have been pastoring and mentoring you and helping your walk with Yeshua.

And though YHVH give you the bread of adversity, and the water of affliction, yet shall not your teachers be removed into a corner any more, but your eyes shall see your teachers: And your ears shall hear a word behind thee, saying, This is the way, walk ye in it, when ye turn to the right hand, and when ye turn to the left.

—Isaiah 30:20,21

Ask them to forgive you and release you from the debt that you owe. Most of them will forgive you and release you from the restitution and from paying back tithes; some may not. But whatever the case, if you make things right with them and they bless you, you will be free from the curse mentioned in Malachi 3:8, and you will be able to start a new chapter in your life. A chapter of honor and Holy Giving, obedience, favor, blessing and *greatness*. HaleluYah!!!

Whoever then annuls one of the least of these commandments, and teaches others to do the same, shall be called least in the kingdom of heaven; but whoever keeps and teaches them, he shall be called great in the kingdom of heaven.

—Matthew 5:19

WELCOME TO SPIRITUAL & FINANCIAL FREEDOM!

So Yeshua was saying to those Jews who had believed Him, "If you continue in My word, then you are truly disciples of Mine; and you will know the truth, and the truth will make you free.

—John 8:31, 32

Chapter 3

The Third Year Tithe

*When you have finished setting aside a tenth
of all your produce in the third year, the year
of the tithe, you shall give it to the Levite, the
foreigner, the fatherless and the widow, so that
they may eat in your towns and be satisfied.*
—Deuteronomy 26:12

L et us remember that there are four categories of giving: Prescribed giving, Freewill giving, Sacrificial giving and Restitution giving. In the Prescribed Giving, there are *three* categories of tithes:

1. The First Tithe – Belongs in its entirety to the Levites (Leviticus 27:30-32

2. The Third Year Tithe – It is shared between the Levites, the widow, the orphan and the stranger (Deuteronomy 26:12)

3. The Feast Tithe – It is shared between you, your family and servants and the officiating Levites. (Deuteronomy 14:22-27)

We have spoken about the *first tithe* given to the Levites in its entirety (Chapter 2), and in Chapter 4, we will speak of the second tithe or *feast tithe*. Now we will speak about the third year tithe.

The Third Year Tithe

When you have finished setting aside a tenth of all your produce in the third year, the year of the tithe, you shall give it to the Levite, the foreigner, the fatherless and the widow, so that they may eat in your towns and be satisfied.

—Deuteronomy 26:12

The third year tithe is shared between the Levites, the widow, the orphan and the stranger. I call these "alms." Even in the alms that are majorly for the poor, we are to put the Levites/servants of Yah (God) *first*. So the first portion of the alms is to be given to needy Levites that you know. They don't have to necessarily be your mentors in this case. These Levites can be a missionary that you desire to support or a struggling minister in your area and then to the poor, the orphan, the widow and the stranger that are not Levites or not in the ministry. So you first take care of the poor that are in the ministry of YHVH and then the poor that are not in the ministry!

Then you shall give it to the Levite, to the stranger, to the orphan and to the widow, that they may eat in your towns and be satisfied.

—Deuteronomy 26:12b

There are ancient writings that talk about the existence of three tithes that were prescribed in ancient Israel.

"Besides those two tithes, which I have already said you are to pay every year, the one for the Levites, the other for the festivals, you are to bring every third year, a third tithe to be distributed to those that want" (Antiquities of the Jews. Book IV, Chapter VIII, Paragraph 22).

Another secular writer confirmed this as it is written in Tobit 1:6- 8 (an ancient non-canonical book):

"Taking the first fruits and the tithes of my produce and the first shearings, I would give these to the priests, the sons of Aaron, at the altar. Of all my produce I would give a tenth to the sons of Levi who ministered at Jerusalem; a second tenth I would sell, and I would go and spend the proceeds each year at Jerusalem; the third tenth I would give to those to whom it was my duty."

At the end of every third year you shall bring out all the tithe of your produce in that year, and shall deposit it in your town.
—Deuteronomy 14:28

Notice that every three years, all of Israel needed to give an additional tithe to the poor (a third tithe), starting with the poor ministers and then all the other poor and needy of the people. When we give to the poor, orphan and widow as prescribed, we can ask Yah (God) to bless us!

Then shall you say before YHVH your Elohim: 'I have removed the holy tithe from my house, and have given them to the Levite, the stranger, the fatherless, and the widow, according to all Your commandments which you have commanded me: "Look down from Your holy habitation and bless Your people Israel and the land which you have given us, just as you swore to our fathers, a land flowing with milk and honey."'
—Deuteronomy 26:12-15

GIVING THE THIRD YEAR TITHE MONTHLY A 3.33%

Instead of waiting to give an additional tithe at the end of every third year or on the third and the sixth year of a seven-year cycle, we prescribe separating it *monthly* in the following manner:

If your wages are $1,000 a month, then your first tithe to the Levites will be $100, your second tithe for celebrating the feasts will be another $100, and your third tithe would be

$33.3 or 1/3 of a tithe (3.33%) as it is prescribed only once every three years. You could technically begin to count years and separate it all every three years, but I prefer it monthly as it helps me to always have something to give to the poor and needy.

SHABBAT YEAR

Notice that in a seven-year cycle, we need to give the third tithe on the 3rd and 6th year. The Seventh or Shabbat Year is a year of provision and sharing without limitations.

But during the seventh year let the land lie unplowed and unused. Then the poor among your people may get food from it, and the wild animals may eat what is left. Do the same with your vineyard and your olive grove.

—Exodus 23:11

During the Shabbat Years, as during the Shabbat Days, YHVH provides while we *rest*!

Of course, this blessing can be enjoyed only by those who celebrate Shabbat and who honor the Seventh Year of Land and personal rest. Yes! It requires faith to do that! (Hebrews 11:6)

Want to Give More to the Poor?

You can definitely decide to give more than what is prescribed to the poor as the Holy Spirit leads you, but I would not suggest giving any less than that bare minimum.

He who shuts his ear to the cry of the poor will also cry himself and not be answered.

—Proverbs 21:13

If we have already distributed our alms and we have nothing left to give for the poor, it is important to pray and seek Yah (God) in case He wants us to "lend Him some money!"

One who is gracious to a poor man lends to YHVH, And He will repay him for his good deed.

—Proverbs 19:17

If you feel led to give over and above the prescribed alms or "third year tithe," YHVH promises to repay you.

There are situations when a member of our own family (our own flesh) is in need, and that requires us to pray and seek Yah on how we should help; this may be a requirement over and above the prescribed alms! It could be a member of our "spiritual family" as well!

Is it not to divide your bread with the hungry and bring the homeless poor into the house; When you see the naked, to cover him; And not to hide yourself from your own flesh?

—Isaiah 58:7

An Important Warning

There are two kinds of extremes in giving to the poor:

- Not giving at all and being very insensitive to their suffering.
- Giving everything out of false compassion

The first person that does not give falls under a terrible curse. His prayers will not be answered.

He who shuts his ear to the cry of the poor will also cry himself and not be answered.

—Proverbs 21:13

The second person who gives too much can feel abused because God does not give him/her enough for their own needs. Actually, what happened here is that you gave to the poor without taking into consideration your own family needs and the first tithe to the Levites or your pastors/mentors in the Word. You thought that you were doing a good thing, but you actually were mistakenly, out of a good heart, doing "your own thing," so you become poor!

Yeshua corrected Judas Iscariot when Judas rebuked Mary Magdalene for pouring all the expensive perfume on Yeshua instead of giving the proceeds to the poor.

While He was in Bethany at the home of Simon the leper and reclining at the table, there came a woman with an alabaster vial of very costly perfume of pure nard; and she broke the vial and poured it over His head. But some were indignantly remarking to one another, "Why has this perfume been wasted? For this perfume might have been sold for over three hundred denarii, and the money given to the poor." And they were scolding her. But Yeshua said, "Let her alone; why do you bother her? She has done a good deed to Me. For you always have the poor with you, and whenever you wish you can do good to them; but you do not always have Me."

—Mark 14:3-7

Yeshua explained that we should not put the poor above loving Him and when we love Him, we also bless those who teach the Word to us. So do not give to the poor at the expense of other important matters such as blessing your mentors and feeding your family! In fact, in some cases, by blessing the Servants of Yah (God) first, you will put yourself in a position to receive supernatural provision and blessing like in the case of the poor widow and Elijah. (1 Kings 17)

Elijah said to her, "Don't be afraid. Go home and do as you have said. But first make a small loaf of bread for me from what you have and bring it to me, and then make something for yourself and your son. 14 For this is what YHVH, the God of Israel, says: 'the jar of flour will not be used up and the jug of oil will not run dry until the day the LORD *sends rain on the land.'*

—1 Kings 17:13,14

IN SHORT

The third year tithes are alms to be given to the poor and needy, starting with poor Levites (preachers, missionaries, etc.), then the poor in your congregation, then other poor. You can decide to give it as money or as food.

There will always be poor people in the land. Therefore I command you to be openhanded toward your fellow Israelites who are poor and needy in your land.

— Deuteronomy 15:11

How Do You Determine Who Is Really Poor?

But if we have food and clothing, we will be content with that.

—1 Timothy 6:8

We live in a consumer society, so going back to the basics: a person that has no place to stay or money to rent one, no food or no clothing, is considered poor. Of course, we must take into consideration his/her ability to work, and we must enable the poor and encourage them to work and provide. We may help a needy brother or sister with food and clothing and even with shelter, always looking to enable them to come out of their poverty and even teach them to sow financially in their poverty; like the widow who gave the mite into the Temple treasuries for the sustenance of the Levites!

As the well-known popular proverb goes, "What is better? To feed someone with fish or to teach them to fish?"

In most cases, if you have trustworthy leadership, it is advisable to bring the third tithe to your congregation as the pastor should know who the needy people are—the orphans and the widows among you.

Getting Rid of the Curse of Poverty

In order to get rid of the curse of poverty, there is a great promise that we should stand on.

However, there need be no poor people among you, for in the land YHVH your Elohim is giving you to possess as your inheritance, he will richly bless you.

—Deuteronomy 15:4

This powerful promise was fulfilled during the time of the early Jewish apostles in Jerusalem 2,000 years ago!

All the believers were one in heart and mind. No one claimed that any of their possessions was their own, but they shared everything they had. With great power the apostles continued to testify to the resurrection of the LORD Yeshua. And God's grace was so powerfully at work in them all that there were no needy persons among them. For from time to time those who owned land or houses sold them, brought the money from the sales and put it at the apostles' feet, and it was distributed to anyone who had need.

—Acts 4:32-35

The restoration of the true apostolic ministry needs to lead to a place of abundance and blessing where no one lacks anything. The restoration of the apostolic Jewish roots of the faith and the uprooting of replacement theology from every church and congregation should lead to true unity and the banishment of the spirit of poverty and lack, especially when those congregations rise up to bless Israel in action!

Chapter 4

The Feast Tithes

At that time they will call Jerusalem 'The
Throne of the Lord,' and all nations will gather
in Jerusalem to honor the name of YHVH.
No longer will they follow the stubbornness of
their evil hearts.
—Jeremiah 3:17

L et us remember that there are four categories of giving: Prescribed giving, Freewill giving, Sacrificial giving and Restitution giving. In the Prescribed Giving, there are
three categories of tithes:

1. The First Tithe – Belongs in its entirety to the Levites
   (Leviticus 27:30-32)
2. The Third Year Tithe – It is shared between the Levites,
   the widow, the orphan and the stranger (Deuteronomy
   26:12)

3. The Feast Tithe – It is shared between you, your family and servants and the officiating Levites. (Deuteronomy 14:22-27)

We have spoken about the *first tithe* given to the Levites in its entirety (Chapter 2) and the third year tithe that is shared between the Levites, the widow, orphan and stranger. In this chapter, we will speak of the second tithe or *feast tithe.*

Feast Tithe or the Second Tithe

Eat the tithe of your grain, new wine and olive oil, and the firstborn of your herds and flocks in the presence of the LORD your God at the place he will choose as a dwelling for his Name, so that you may learn to revere the LORD your God always.

—Deuteronomy 14:23

This particular tithe is very exciting. It is a personal "savings account" for Holy Days and for prescribed celebrations! Three times a year, all of Israel was summoned to come to celebrate Holy Feasts and Convocations (*Moadim*) in Jerusalem.

Three times a year all your men must appear before the LORD your God at the place He will choose: at the Festival of Unleavened Bread, the Festival of Weeks and the Festival of Tabernacles. No one should appear before the LORD empty- handed: Each of you must bring a gift in proportion to the way the LORD your God has blessed you.

—Deuteronomy 16:16,17

Our Elohim is a marvelous father, and when He calls us to worship and celebrate Him, He wants to make sure that we *enjoy* it! How sad it would be if we need to enjoy a festival and we have no money to pay for the hotel, for the food and for the activities? How much rejoicing would there be if our pockets are empty when our children ask us for ice cream or some trinket to buy?

Use the silver to buy whatever you like: cattle, sheep, wine or other fermented drink, or anything you wish. Then you and your household shall eat there in the presence of the LORD your God and rejoice.

—Deuteronomy 16:26

On top of it, He wants us to have enough money to give to the Levites officiating in the Temple. We should never appear with empty hands when we go worship the Almighty! So the feast tithe is the God-given insurance that we will have enough money for ourselves and for our families when celebrating Him and also enough to give to the Levites that officiate or that minister.

And do not neglect the Levites living in your towns, for they have no allotment or inheritance of their own.

—Deuteronomy 16:27

Feast Tithes In a Modern-Day Society

Since YHVH is an up-to-date Elohim and His name means the I AM, we know that by His Ruach (Spirit), we can know how to relate to this tithe. One important question arises here: Are all the believers in the world supposed to come to Jerusalem to celebrate the feasts? After all, this tithe is for the purpose of celebrating the Holy Feasts of Pessach, Shavuot and Sukkot in Jerusalem. That is easy when you are an Israeli living in His Land, but what about someone from Australia? Is Yah (God) really expecting people from the ends of the earth to come to Israel to celebrate the feasts? Can't we celebrate them in our nations instead?

The Word of God is very clear about the call of the Gentiles to come to Jerusalem:

This is what the LORD *Almighty says: "Many peoples and the inhabitants of many cities will yet come, 21 and the inhabitants of one city will go to another and say, 'Let us go at once to entreat YHVH and seek the* LORD *Almighty. I myself am going.' 22 And many peoples and powerful nations will come to Jerusalem to seek the* LORD *Almighty and to entreat him."*

—Zechariah 8:20-22

It is a Holy Mandate and a sign of great honor to the God of Israel when nations come to seek Him in Jerusalem and when they do, they are amply rewarded with *answered prayer* and *miracles*!

As for the foreigner who does not belong to your people Israel but has come from a distant land because of Your great name and Your mighty hand and Your outstretched arm—*when they come and pray toward this temple, then hear from heaven, your dwelling place.* Do whatever the foreigner asks of You, so that all the peoples of the earth may know Your name and fear You, as do your own people Israel, and may know that this house I have built bears Your Name.

—2 Chronicles 6:32,33

But can't I pray in my own city? Why do I need to seek God in Jerusalem? Aren't all places the same? The Word says that He has exalted Jerusalem *above* all other cities and Israel above all other nations.

In the last days the mountain of the YHVH's temple will be established as the highest of the mountains; it will be exalted above the hills, and all nations will stream to it.

—Isaiah 2:1,2

Most of us would agree that we are in the *last days*, is it not? Well, the greatest miracle of the last days is the restoration of Israel and the *return* of the Jewish people to their promised land—Israel (*aliyah*), as prophesied by numerous biblical prophets (Ezekiel 26:24-28, Amos 9, Isaiah 66 and many more). Since then (14th of May 1948), we entered into the last days, and indeed YHVH is establishing Israel in a miraculous

way and exalting Jerusalem that is called to be the Throne of
ADONAI!

At that time they will call Jerusalem The Throne of the LORD,
and all nations will gather in Jerusalem to honor the name of
YHVH. No longer will they follow the stubbornness of their evil
hearts.

—Jeremiah 3:17

So, to the original question: Are believers from all nations
called to come up to Zion, to Israel, to celebrate YHVH's Holy
Feasts and honor His name? The answer is a resolute *yes*!

Moreover, the Word of God tells us that those nations that
do not come to celebrate the Feast of Sukkot (Tabernacles) in
Jerusalem will have no rain, no food and no prosperity. Rain
also symbolizes *revival*, so I would say *no revival*!

If any of the peoples of the earth do not go up to Jerusalem to
worship the King, the LORD Almighty, they will have no rain.
18 If the Egyptian people do not go up and take part, they will
have no rain. The LORD will bring on them the plague he
inflicts on the nations that do not go up to celebrate the Festival
of Tabernacles.

—Zechariah 14:17-18

The Feast Tithe Enables You to Come Up to Zion

When you follow the prescribed commandment in the Torah
to separate the feast tithe, you will have enough money to come
to Israel to celebrate the feasts. Maybe you will not be able to

come three times a year, but if you are faithful to save the feast tithes, you may be able to come once a year. Some may be able to come once in a few years! But I have seen many miracles released to those that take the step of faith to come even if they do not have enough money. And if you can't come, go ahead and support your pastor to come, sow your feast tithes to enable others to come!

Let me tell you something: The moment that you begin to separate the feast tithes in order to come up to Jerusalem to celebrate any of His feasts, you will be able to experience amazing financial breakthroughs. Yes, you will see that your money that is left from giving the *three* prescribed tithes and the first fruits offerings will go beyond its real value. You will see miracles of provision like never before! When you follow Yah's (God's) financial system, you will be in His hands for provision. Not in the hands of your boss or your business but in His hands, and when He is your shepherd, you will not lack.

YHVH is my shepherd, I lack nothing.

—Psalms 23:1

He is our Shepherd when we *follow* Him and His instructions in righteousness and the right way of living and *giving*!

Start putting aside all of your tithes: *The first* (to the Levites), *the second (feasts in Jerusalem), the third* (3% for the poor and needy) and you will see a shift in your spiritual wellbeing that will be followed by your financial wellbeing as well!

When we live according to Yah's ways and commandments, we live on the edge, which means that we need to trust Him and not our money that we have or do not have. That is a great antidote against unbelief and the love of Mammon which is the root of all evil. When we are free from the love of Mammon because we obey Him in the *giving* arena, we will then be ready to receive *the blessing*!

The prescribed giving in the Torah is based on the following two Royal Commandments:

Yeshua replied: "'Love the LORD *your God with all your heart and with all your soul and with all your mind.' This is the first and greatest commandment. And the second is like it: 'Love your neighbour as yourself.' All the Law and the Prophets hang on these two commandments."*

—Matthew 22:38, 39

When we give the first fruits to the Cohanim (Priests) and the *first tithe* to the Levites, we are loving Elohim-God *first* (above our neighbor or ourselves). That is the antidote against idolatry.

When we give the third year tithe (3% per month) to the Levite and the poor, we are still loving God *first* (Levite) and also our neighbor (widows, orphans and strangers).

When we separate our feast tithes to celebrate the feasts of YHVH in Jerusalem, we love Yah (God) first as we come to celebrate Him in His Land (blessing his ministers first) and also have enough money for ourselves to spend and to enjoy a

Holy Vacation. So the second tithe causes us to love Him and ourselves. Praise Yah!

Indeed functioning in Holy Giving is an issue of the heart. If we *love* the Almighty, our neighbor and ourselves, it will show in our *obedience* to *Holy Giving*!

How is your heart and your love life doing? If not so good, then it is time to *repent*, *return* and be *restored*. Remember that Holy Giving requires *faith*, and without faith, we cannot please Yah (God).

And without faith it is impossible to please God, because anyone who comes to him must believe that he exists and that he rewards those who earnestly seek him.

—Hebrews 11:6

When you put aside your feast tithes in order to come up to Jerusalem to honor Him and to honor His people Israel, He Himself will release the blessing of the Key of Abraham over your life!

"I will bless those who bless you"

—Genesis 12:3

Chapter 5

Righteous Giving – Righteous Living

*Riches do not profit in the day of wrath, but
righteousness delivers from death.*
—Proverbs 11:4

The Eternal Word of Elohim tells us that the center of all our lives is our hearts. Whatever is in the heart of a human being will also direct all his thoughts, speech and ultimately his actions. Giving and obedience to the Almighty, hence a righteous lifestyle, is a matter of the heart. There is a direct connection between a Giving Heart and a Righteous Heart! It is so closely related that the Hebrew word for Righteous Giving is exactly the same word for Righteous Living.

Zedaka

The word *Zedaka* comes from the word *zedek*, which means *justice*. A just man is called a *zadik*. When the Hebrew talks about "walking in righteousness" or being just, it is totally connected with the way you lead your financial affairs in the area of *giving*.

I have been young and now I am old, yet I have not seen the righteous forsaken or his descendants begging bread. All day long he is gracious and lends, and his descendants are a blessing.

—Psalms 37:25,26

A righteous man is described as one that "lends" or gives all day long, and because of that *righteousness* (of *giving*), he is blessed, and his descendants are a blessing!

Righteous Giving Delivers From Death

One of the most common beliefs among the Orthodox Jews is that giving to someone that prays for you or teaches you Torah and to the poor is *life insurance* better than any life insurance you may take and *pay* for.

Riches do not profit in the day of wrath, but righteousness delivers from death.

—Proverbs 11:4

The word used here for *righteousness* is *zedaka* which also means *righteous giving* or *just giving*. Notice that this verse is in the context of *riches* that do not profit in the day of wrath, adversity or trouble. The right translation would have been as follows:

"RICHES DO NOT PROFIT IN THE DAY OF WRATH, BUT *RIGHTEOUS GIVING* DELIVERS FROM DEATH"

In the first four chapters of *focus on Holy Giving*, I taught you about "prescribed giving": about the first fruits and the three tithes—that is *righteous giving*!

As we study Proverbs 11 to the end, we will see that this is the predominant subject of this proverb as it is in many others.

The wicked earns deceptive wages, but he who sows righteousness gets a true reward.

—Proverbs 11:18

Again, notice that the context of this verse above is about *money*, so the whole verse is in that context. Again the word for *righteousness* is *zedaka* which also means *righteous giving,* and of course, it is about *sowing*.

So let us translate it correctly from the Hebrew now:

The wicked earns deceptive wages, but he who sows righteously, giving what is prescribed, *gets a true reward!*

In other words, if you are not sowing financially what is prescribed, do not expect a reward. So the difference between the wicked and the righteous here is in the way that each one relates to *money* and *possessions*. One pursues after it, doing anything to get money or "deceptive wages." The wicked perverts himself if need be just to get the money, but the Righteous *gives* in a just, right and holy way as YHVH has prescribed in His Torah and therefore gets a reward. HaleluYah! These are *great news*!

To make sure that we understand this point, the writer of the Proverbs emphasizes:

There is one who scatters, and yet increases all the more, and there is one who withholds what is justly due, and yet it results only in want.

—Proverbs 11:24

What is *justly due*? Please refer to my first four chapters on Focus on Holy Giving and you will learn about prescribed giving, which is *justly due*.

Now you can understand the very well-known Scriptures in Malachi when YHVH calls Israel to attention.

'Will a man rob God? Yet you are robbing Me! But you say, "How have we robbed You?" In tithes and offerings. You are cursed with a curse, for you are robbing Me, the whole nation of you!'

—Malachi 3:8,9

Withholding the first fruits offerings, the three tithes and other required offerings are called *"Robbing Elohim-God"* or "withholding what is *justly due*," and that brings the *curse* on.

A MATTER OF THE HEART

Why is it that the Almighty is so "touchy" about *righteous giving*? Because it is a matter of the heart. If you are not a righteous giver, your heart is totally sick and full of darkness! Many Christians/Messianics have a pseudo-spiritual life. They even pray and speak the right lingo, but until they obey Elohim in the *giving* arena, their hearts don't really belong to him. This is *very clear*!

For where your treasure is, there your heart will be also.
—Matthew 6:21

The heart is more deceitful than all else and is desperately sick; Who can understand it?
—Jeremiah 17:9

If they resent *giving* as Yah (God) prescribed, their hearts are bound in iniquity and the love of Mammon, which is the root of *all* evil.

For the love of money is a root of all kinds of evil. Some people, eager for money, have wandered from the faith and pierced themselves with many griefs.
—1 Timothy 6:10

This goes for the poor and the rich alike. *Righteous giving* will rescue a poor person from their poverty! Anyone poor or rich that will begin to obey in the area of *righteous giving* will come out of poverty sooner or later! Sometimes, you will have to persevere until the Word manifests, but it will manifest if you continue in *obedience*.

"Test me in this," says the LORD Almighty, "and see if I will not throw open the floodgates of heaven and pour out so much blessing that there will not be room enough to store it.

—Malachi 3:11

The Eternal Word of God is totally clear about this: A person that is righteous in his giving will also be righteous in their living because their hearts (and treasure) will be in the right place. If your heart is in the right place in the issue of Righteous Giving, it will also be in the right place concerning other things. If there is no *lust* in your heart for money, there will be no lust for illicit sex, no coveting or envy; you will lead a Holy Life. That is why the *first* Issue of *repentance* or *returning* unto Elohim-God and His Ways is in *giving*!

"I YHVH do not change. So you, the descendants of Jacob, are not destroyed. 7 Ever since the time of your ancestors you have turned away from my decrees and have not kept them. Return to me, and I will return to you," says the LORD Almighty. "But you ask, 'How are we to return?' "Will a mere mortal rob God? Yet you rob me. "But you ask, 'How are we robbing you?' In tithes and offerings."

—Malachi 3:6-8

When we truly do *Teshuva* (*repent* and *return*), the first thing that will manifest is a willingness to *give* to obey Elohim in the giving arena! Notice that it is not any kind of giving but in *tithes and offerings*.

So, if you are bound up in iniquity and you have strongholds in your life you can't get rid of, you know what to do! Repent from robbing the Almighty and start to *give* according to what is prescribed (first fruits, three tithes) and according to what the Holy Spirit on top of it puts in your heart (voluntary, sacrificial or restitution giving). As you do *Teshuva* (repent) on this issue, you will also experience deliverance in all other areas of your life, for *righteous giving* always leads to *righteous living*!

The one who receives instruction in the Word should share all good things with their instructor. Do not be deceived: God cannot be mocked. A man reaps what he sows. Whoever sows to please their flesh, from the flesh will reap destruction; whoever sows to please the Spirit, from the Spirit will reap eternal life.

—Galatians 6:6,7

The writer of Galatians, the Apostle Paul, said clearly that withholding what is rightly due from those who teach the Word to you, your pastors, bishops and mentors will cause you to go into *corruption*. For instead of sowing and giving righteously, you invest in yourself only!

Whoever sows to please their flesh, from the flesh will reap destruction; whoever sows to please the Spirit, from the Spirit will reap eternal life.

—Galatians 6:7

Watch over your heart in this matter as the heart is *desperately sick*; pray about this seriously and change your ways! No doubt you will have a breakthrough. Be faithful at it *all of your life*! This will be your *life insurance* and your *sure reward*.

Watch over your heart with all diligence, for from it flow the springs of life.

—Proverbs 4:23

There is no way to walk in the blessing, the anointing of abundant life both spiritually and materially but through *righteous giving*.

ZEDAKA!

Those who trust in their riches will fall, but the righteous (who practice Righteous Giving) will thrive like a green leaf.

—Proverbs 11:28

Chapter 6

Priestly Giving

And, so to speak, through Abraham even Levi,
who received tithes, paid tithes.
—Hebrews 7:9

As I endeavor to give you the Biblical perspective on *giving*, I do so with fear and trembling. There have been a lot of abuses done in the name of "giving" and lots of manipulation. But where there are abuses and extremes, there is also *truth* somewhere that needs to be recovered, for as we all know, only the knowledge of the truth can make us *free*!

And you shall know the truth, and the truth shall make you free.
—John 8:32

In the first five chapters, I have written about *giving* in general as prescribed by the Eternal Word of Elohim. We have spoken about the *three tithes* and the *first fruits offerings*. We have seen that it is very serious to owe God money! We also mentioned that all the tithes and first fruits offerings are to be given to the Levites and the Priests who are Yah's (God's) ministers besides the third year tithe that belongs *both* to the Levites and to the widow, orphan and the stranger. So by now, we know that the ministers of Elohim-God are commanded to receive tithes from the people (that are not in the full-time ministry.)

And verily they that are of the sons of Levi, who receive the office of the priesthood, have a commandment to take tithes of the people according to the law, that is, of their brethren, though they come out of the loins of Abraham.

—Hebrews 7:5

Why is it that the priests and Levites are *commanded to take tithes from the people*? (In other words, not taking the tithes would be breaking Yah's (God's) Commandments.) the reason is that the Levites have no inheritance besides the *Priesthood*!

For the Levites have no portion among you, because the priesthood of YHVH is their inheritance.

—Joshua 18:7

While the rest of Israel could dedicate themselves to their own business and family affairs, the priests need to be dedicated to the Priesthood. The life of a minister is a life of whole devotion to *serving* the Almighty and His people. So rightly so, the people are *commanded* to support them and honor them with their tithes and offerings!

Only the Levites shall perform the service of the tent of meeting, and they shall bear their iniquity; it shall be a perpetual statute throughout your generations, and among the sons of Israel, they shall have no inheritance. For the tithe of the sons of Israel, which they offer as an offering to YHVH, I have given to the Levites for an inheritance; *therefore I have said concerning them, 'They shall have no inheritance among the sons of Israel.'*
—Numbers 18:23,24

On top of the *tithes* and *offerings*, the people were *commanded* to give the Levites cities and lands to live in!

Command the sons of Israel that they give to the Levites from the inheritance of their possession cities to live in; and you shall give to the Levites pasture lands around the cities.
—Numbers 35:2

So the sons of Israel gave the Levites from their inheritance these cities with their pasture lands, according to the command of YHVH.
—Joshua 21:3

When was the last time you asked YHVH about your lands and houses and which portion belongs to the Levite-Minister that ministers to you? Why is it that throughout the body of Messiah, (the church) people are expecting Yah's ministers to "manage on their own"?

The Levitical priests, the whole tribe of Levi, shall have no portion or inheritance with Israel; they shall eat YHVH'S offerings by fire and His portion.

—Deuteronomy 18:1

How can they manage on their own if their lives are poured out on the altar for *service*? That's the reason why so many wonderful ministers are suffering need. And of course, if the ministers are suffering, it brings a *curse* upon the entire Body!

Will a man rob God? Yet ye have robbed me. But ye say, wherein have we robbed thee? In tithes and offerings. Ye are cursed with a curse: for ye have robbed me, even this whole nation.

—Malachi 3:8,9 KJV

This is confirmed in the Book of Galatians in the New Covenant. ADONAI will bless the rest of the Body according to how we behave with His ministers concerning *giving*. The Word admonishes each person to provide for himself and not to put a strain on others financially. People are commanded to work, provide and *give* and not to become a burden on others. However, when it comes to the teachers and ministers of the Word, all are commanded to *give* financially to them just like the Torah prescribes!

For each one should carry their own load. Nevertheless, the one who receives instruction in the Word should share all good things with their instructor.

—Galatians 6:5,6

When we do not take care of those who instruct us in the Word, we are *mocking God,* and He calls us *"deceived"*!!! I believe that this is the major reason for both spiritual and financial poverty in the Body of Yeshua.

Do not be deceived: God cannot be mocked. A man reaps what he sows. Whoever sows to please their flesh, from the flesh will reap destruction; whoever sows to please the Spirit, from the Spirit will reap eternal life.

—Galatians 6:7,8

It is no surprise, therefore, that Elohim says, "Test Me on this"!

Bring the whole tithe into the storehouse, so that there may be food in My house, and test Me now in this," says the LORD of hosts, "if I will not open for you the windows of heaven and pour out for you a blessing until it overflows.

—Malachi 3:10

Please notice that these *tithes* are not for *"projects"* and *"building funds."* This money is for the Levites' *personal provision.* When you give your tithes and first fruits to the "ministry," it is to the *minister* of the *ministry* that you are giving it to. It is to his/her discretion how much they decide to keep or to give, and we will see this later on in this chapter. Tithes and *first fruits* are *not* for projects or building funds, they are for *people,* for Yeshua's ministers that labor day and night for Him, for *you* and for lost souls. They *deserve* to be royally provided for! They have no "working hours"; their whole life is a sacrifice.

On that day men were also appointed over the chambers for the stores, the contributions, the first fruits and the tithes, to gather into them from the fields of the cities the portions required by the law for the priests and Levites; for Judah rejoiced over the priests and Levites who served.

—Nehemiah 12:44

No Tithes, No Ministers

When the Levites/ministers do not receive the tithes, they leave the ministry! That leaves a terrible spiritual vacuum, and it brings about darkness! It is like leaving a garden without tending and it grows weed, thorns and briers! That is what the Kehila (Church) looks like when the ministers leave their post for lack of provision!

I also discovered that the portions of the Levites had not been given them, so that the Levites and the singers who performed the service had gone away, each to his own field.

—Nehemiah 13:10

I can tell you from my own experience that there were years that we suffered terribly because the believers did not know about giving. We really tried to find all kinds of solutions and considered going into business. We even tried Network Marketing one year, thinking that we could combine the ministry with it! Very soon, we discovered that there was *no way* to keep the integrity of the ministry and keep on in business! If all of our time, thoughts and being are *busy* trying to provide, we cannot have the presence of mind, heart and spirit to be filled with the Word in prayer!

But we will devote ourselves to prayer and to the ministry of the Word.

—Acts 6:4

Some people even judged us for going into business, but they had no business doing so since they never sent their tithes and offerings to *support* us, so we did not need to try other things for provision! We never left the ministry but tried to balance both and chose to stay in the ministry (though we were fast becoming some of the most successful in the marketing company!). When we chose to stay in the ministry, we still kept on suffering lack and getting into credit card debt to continue living and ministering! That beloved is because most people in the body of Messiah are *mocking God* as Galatians 6:7 also says!

For each one should carry their own load. Nevertheless, the one who receives instruction in the Word should share all good things with their instructor.

—Galatians 6:5,6

What are these "GOOD THINGS?" The three tithes and first fruits and other free will offerings! (See previous five chapters!)

Priestly Giving – Tithe of Tithes

Until now, we have spoken about Holy Giving as pertaining to most of the Body of Yeshua (church) that is *not* in *full-time* ministry! We are fully aware that many people exercise their gifts and do some ministry. We are *all* called to be witnesses; however, only a *few* are called to the Five Fold Ministry. Only *"some"* are called to devote themselves wholly to Yah's (God's) Service!

And He gave some as apostles, and some as prophets, and some as evangelists, and some as pastors and teachers, for the equipping of the saints for the work of service, to the building up of the body of Messiah.

—Ephesians 4:11,12

In the Greek Language, the word "some" is a *neuter* gender; in other words, it implies *men* and *women*!

So, we can see that the modern-day Levites are those Five Fold ministers that devote themselves to His service, and their portion is the tithes and offerings from the rest of the people!

The Levitical priests, the whole tribe of Levi, shall have no portion or inheritance with Israel; they shall eat YHVH'S offerings by fire and His portion.

—Deuteronomy 18:1

And How should the Ministers of Elohim-God Give?

The Torah instructs the Levites to give a tithe of the tithe!

Moreover, you shall speak to the Levites and say to them, 'When you take from the sons of Israel the tithe which I have given you from them for your inheritance, then you shall present an offering from it to YHVH, a tithe of the tithe.

—Numbers 18:26

So the ministers are called to give only *one* tithe; that is what I call "The Priestly Tithe."

So you shall also present an offering to YHVH from your tithes, which you receive from the sons of Israel; and from it you shall give YHVH'S offering to Aaron the priest.

—Numbers 18:28

That tithe is to be given to Aaron the High Priest. Practically speaking, most ministers of Yeshua have a pastor or a teacher that blesses them, that helps or helped mentor them. This Tithe of Tithes is to be sent to them!

The priest, the son of Aaron, shall be with the Levites when the Levites receive tithes, and the Levites shall bring up the tenth of the tithes to the house of our God, to the chambers of the storehouse.

—Nehemiah 10:38

And what happens if a minister does not have such a mentor but rather a few different ones? Then my suggestion is that they seek Yah (God) about whom to give the Tithe of Tithes to.

Share it among your different mentors, maybe other ministers that are struggling, and especially why not bless the ministers in Israel? After all, the nations have received the Word and the gospel from Israel, and they are indebted!

For Macedonia and Achaia have been pleased to make a contribution for the poor among the saints in Jerusalem. Yes, they were pleased to do so, and they are indebted to them. For if the Gentiles have shared in their spiritual things, they are indebted to minister to them also in material things.

—Romans 15:26, 27

After searching the Scriptures, I have come to the conclusion that full-time ministers are only commanded to bring the Tithe of Tithes to Yah (God). The rest is to their discretion! How much they decide to give to the poor or to other ministers, peoples and projects is according to their integrity and their discretion.

And, so to speak, through Abraham even Levi, who received tithes, paid tithes.

—Hebrews 7:9

There was a time when the Kehila (church) in Jerusalem brought *all* that they had, and they put it at the Apostles' feet. In this case, it was not just *prescribed* tithes and offerings but actually *all*! That, of course, caused the Apostles to become stewards and *funnels* through which the Blessing is distributed to others! Nevertheless, how much and to who they distributed was left to the Apostles' discretion and leading!

For there was not a needy person among them, for all who were owners of land or houses would sell them and bring the proceeds of the sales and lay them at the apostles' feet, and they would be distributed to each as any had need.

—Acts 4:34

In order to sum it all up:

1. The ministers of Yeshua are entitled and commanded to receive tithes and offerings from the rest of the Body!
2. If Levites/ministers are not provided for, they are in danger of leaving the ministry.
3. Tithes, first fruits and some other prescribed offerings are for the ministers and not for "projects."
4. Ministry projects and building funds are supported by specific offerings that are "earmarked."
5. If there is such a move like in Acts 4:34 and what they receive is not only tithes and prescribed offerings, but far beyond that, then they also become funnels through which the financial blessing flows to other parts of the Body that are needy!
6. The only financial obligation that a full-time minister has is to give the *Tithe* of *Tithes* to the High Priest Yeshua according to His leading.
7. Ministries in the nations should remember Israel when distributing the Tithe of Tithes.

We believe that all ministries have ministers in them, and when offerings are not earmarked for specific projects, the minister is entitled to use them according to his/her discretion!

So all ministries are called to separate a Tithe of Tithes to give away to others (always taking Israel into consideration when giving!), and the rest is left to the minister and the leadership team's discretion!

We personally suggest that every ministry in the nations will also separate the feast tithes (second tithe; see Chapter 4) and leave it as a saving fund to send their pastor/leader to Israel to celebrate the feasts and to be nourished by the Word from Zion!

For the law will go forth from Zion and the Word of YHVH from Jerusalem.

—Isaiah 2:3b

Chapter 7

Releasing the 1,000 Fold Blessing

Now this I say, he who sows sparingly will also
reap sparingly, and he who sows bountifully
will also reap bountifully.
—2 Corinthians 9:6

Giving and Receiving is like *breathing*. It is part of the rhythm of life and essential to it! If we don't breathe, we do not live on physically. If we do not give, we also die because we are going contrary to God's nature in us. Elohim created us in such a way that everything is in balance. When we breathe, we have to *inhale* and *exhale*. If we only take in the air but do not expel it, we will be choked to death. If we only expel the air but do not take in air, we will die of asphyxia! The same oxygen that is a blessing to us can become a curse if we do not expel the air out! In the same way, if we only get money but do not give, it will kill us spiritually! Even if we get very little money and even if we are poor, we must *give* the little that we can, according to the Word's prescription, so we can have a breakthrough! (2 Corinthians 9:6-8)

Everything in life has the same balanced reciprocity: Giving and receiving, inhaling and exhaling, sowing and reaping and so on. If when we breathe and take air in, we only expel very little air, we will lose our ability to breathe deeply and take in enough air for life! The expelling makes room for more air to come in! In the same way, it is the *sowing* that makes more room for *reaping*!

Now He who supplies seed to the sower and bread for food will supply and multiply your seed for sowing and increase the harvest of your righteousness.

—2 Corinthians 9:10

In the past few chapters, we talked about *Prescribed Giving*, and now we will talk with another type of *giving*, and I will call it Faith Giving. We need faith when we do prescribed giving, of course, and without faith, we cannot even please Yah (God)! (Hebrews 11:6)

Prescribed giving is more predictable, more "orderly." We can time it and plan it, and that is extremely important! However, Faith Giving leads us to sow what I call *potent seeds*. Faith Giving is extremely exciting, and its outcome and results can be tremendously surprising, to say the least!

The Potent Seed

But what is a *potent seed*? The best way to explain it is through the childbearing process. When a man impregnates his wife, the Creator designed *seeds* or sperms. In most cases, when a woman falls pregnant through a natural process (not in vitro fertilization!), she will give birth to *one* child. In some exceptional cases, she may have *twins*. The Bible does not show anything beyond *twins* as there was no "science" at that time that intervened with the natural process that the Creator, God Himself, set up in a human being.

Impregnation occurs when *one potent seed* (one sperm among millions that swim with all their might!) "makes it to target" and penetrates the female ovum (the egg!). The outcome is pregnancy and, eventually, the birthing of a delightful baby! In some exceptional cases, that *one* seed impregnates one ovum that splits into two, and identical twins are created! In other exceptional cases, *two* potent seeds impregnate two eggs, and non-identical twins are created! (Like in the case of Jacob and Esau). Think about it, out of millions of sperm-seed, only *one* or exceptionally *two* manage to cause pregnancy and thus bring forth *fruit*! (babies!)

Be Fruitful & Multiply!

God blessed them; and God said to them, "Be fruitful and multiply, and fill the earth, and subdue it; and rule over the fish of the sea and over the birds of the sky and over every living thing that moves on the earth.

—Genesis 1:28

That is Elohim's first commandment to mankind, and that commandment carries authority into every area of our lives. Be fruitful and multiply in everything, including financially! If you live out of agriculture or livestock, it is good to know that YHVH said to every living thing (not only to Adam) to be fruitful and to multiply! If you have a ministry, it is good to know that the Almighty wants your ministry to be fruitful and to multiply disciples! If you have a business, it is good to know that Abba wants you to be fruitful and multiply finances, branches, franchises, everything that you set your hands to do!

Fruitfulness and multiplication are both a commandment and a *blessing*! If we obey His commandment, then we will also be blessed by it! We have to on purpose, actively seek to become fruitful and to multiply! That will take us out of our comfort zone as we will have to be seeking God on what to do and how to do it in order to fulfill His commandment of fruitfulness and multiplication and to live in the blessing!

We can see that our forefathers Abraham, Isaac and Jacob always *increased*! Their families flourished even in old age with new life (Isaac!), and their businesses of livestock and trading expanded with no limitations. The multiplication was so great that they became a threat to kings and kingdoms!

Now Abram was very rich in livestock, in silver and in gold.

—Genesis 13:2

The same happened to every king in Israel that was faithful to YHVH; the blessing of fruitfulness and multiplication manifested, again and again, interfered only by their own sin or disobedience! In some cases, they were tested like in the case of Joseph and Daniel, but once they passed the test, they always expanded and were the head in every endeavor (even Joseph in jail!).

GIVING A POTENT SEED

When it comes to finances and giving, the principle of the potent seed is the same! First of all, notice that millions of sperm start the race for the egg, and only *one* "makes it to baby"! In the same way, it is extremely important to keep on giving by faith even if you do not see immediate results. Every farmer knows the importance of sowing plenty of seed, for he never knows which one will germinate!

Now this I say, he who sows sparingly will also reap sparingly, and he who sows bountifully will also reap bountifully.
—2 Corinthians 9:6

At the same time, there is a form of giving that is sacrificial, that is extravagant, that will always produce a reaction with the Almighty! We can see this when Miriam from Migdal (Mary Magdalene) poured out the entire costly perfume on the Master!

While He was in Bethany at the home of Simon the leper, and reclining at the table, there came a woman with an alabaster

*vial of very costly perfume of pure nard; and she broke the vial
and poured it over His head.*

—Mark 14:3

Yeshua was so touched that this one act of extravagant
giving made her famous for all generations to come, in spite of
the criticism from Judas Iscariot and the others!

*She has done what she could; she has anointed My body
beforehand for the burial. Truly I say to you,* wherever the
gospel is preached in the whole world, what this woman has
done will also be spoken of in memory of her.

—Mark 14:9, 10

Miriam's extravagant giving gained her *fame* and *favor.*
Later on, we will see that Yeshua goes ahead and raises Miriam's
brother, Lazarus, from the dead.

*It was the Mary who anointed the LORD with ointment, and
wiped His feet with her hair, whose brother Lazarus was sick.*

—John 11:2

He also privileged her to be the *first* person to see the Risen
Messiah! She also became the *first* Preacher of the Resurrection,
and she preached to the Apostles! (A woman!)

*Mary Magdalene came, announcing to the disciples, "I have
seen the LORD," and that He had said these things to her.*

—John 20:18

Her giving or rather pouring of the most expensive perfume that she possessed impacted her life and the life of all of those who follow her example! Often times giving potent seeds will cause historic impact and spiritual reaping for generations to come, like in the case of Miriam!

One Thousand Rams on the Altar

Another potent seed was given by King Solomon to YHVH. Solomon was a very young lad, and he was scared of ruling. He needed Yah's (God's) favor and help desperately! He needed to draw God's attention, and He did it by giving an extravagant sacrifice! He gave burnt offerings which meant he could not take his money back!

The king went to Gibeon to sacrifice there, for that was the great high place; Solomon offered a thousand burnt offerings on that altar.

—1 Kings 3:4

The reaction of the Almighty was a *visitation* with an awesome question: "What do you want, Solomon?"

Can you imagine yourself being visited by the King of the Universe, ready to give you anything you ask? He has the ability to do anything; absolutely *nothing* is impossible for Him! King Solomon asked Him for wisdom to rule all of Israel, and on top of it, YHVH gave him legendary riches.

Behold, I have done according to your words. Behold, I have given you a wise and discerning heart, so that there has been no one like you before you, nor shall one like you arise after you. 13 I have also given you what you have not asked, both riches and honour, so that there will not be any among the kings like you all your day.

—1 Kings 3:12,13

You can never out-give the Almighty; He will always surprise you *big time*! Especially when you give out of *love* and *faith* (not hype, please!), sacrificially, and when He requires you to give something extravagant! Notice that in the case of Miriam (Mary Magdalene) and Solomon, He did not require it of them! Both of them felt the need to express their love to the King of the Universe in extravagant ways! And both of them enjoyed extraordinary attention from El Shaddai! How much more if He speaks to us to give a potent seed?

And *who* did they give this potent seed to? In the case of King Solomon, it was a burnt offering. He gave it to ADONAI on the Altar or the High Place (likened unto the place where you worship or congregational altar!) In the case of Miriam, Yeshua enjoyed the perfume all by Himself as an itinerant preacher and minister! He is the Messiah, of course, but He walked as a prophet, an evangelist, a teacher, a pastor, a preacher and a rabbi! This was an act of extravagant honor to her mentor and deliverer as she did not know at the time that He was Elohim in the flesh. He was her rabbi (teacher), and she called him "my teacher," even at His Resurrection!

Yeshua said to her, "Mary!" She turned and said to Him in Hebrew, "Rabboni!" (which means, Teacher).

—John 20:16

When you sow a potent seed out of extravagant love and faith or out of extravagant obedience, you will never go unnoticed! The fruitfulness, multiplication and blessing that come out of it are unique, history-making and life-changing! Do not let fear stop you from fruitfulness and multiplication!

Now faith is the assurance of things hoped for, the conviction of things not seen. For by it the men of old gained approval.

—Hebrews 11:1

Breathe. Give. Breathe. Receive. Breathe. Give a potent seed...Receive, receive, receive!

Important: remember to declare the Word of God over your circumstances and concerning financial breakthrough.

Death and life are in the power of the tongue, And those who love it will eat its fruit.

—Proverbs 18:21

And according to Mark 11:23-24, you can have whatever you say:

Truly I say to you, whoever says to this mountain, 'Be taken up and cast into the sea,' and does not doubt in his heart, but believes that what he says is going to happen, it will be granted him. Therefore I say to you, all things for which you pray and ask, believe that you have received them, and they will be granted you.

—Mark 11:23-24

Chapter 8

Reaping at the Speed of Light

For a thousand years in Your sight are
like yesterday when it passes by,
or as a watch in the night.
—Psalms 90:4

I was listening to a teaching CD of a known prophetess, intercessor and lover of Israel, Billie Brim, and a tremendous revelation "hit me"! A revelation that will begin to accelerate all that happens in the Spirit:

Reaping at the Speed of Light

In this particular CD, Billie was talking about a song that is sang among the Zulus in Africa called: "Walking in the Light of God" and how they would sing this song even for hours. It is only one sentence based on 1 John 1:5: "*this is the message we have heard from Him and announce to you, that Elohim-God is Light, and in Him, there is no darkness at all."*

When we walk in His Light, no darkness, sin, poverty, disease, etc., can catch up with us! No demon can walk in the Light, so the realm of the Light is the safest place to be and the most effective and blessed!

When we walk in the Light, we can be in unity and have intimate fellowship with one another because we are *one* in the Light, *one* under the Blood!

But if we walk in the Light as He Himself is in the Light, we have fellowship with one another, and the blood of Jesus His Son cleanses us from all sin.

—1 John 1:7

Walking in the Light means walking in truth—His Word all the way from Bereshit (Genesis) and all the Torah to the Book of Revelation

Sanctify them in the truth; Your word is truth. That they may all be one; even as You, Father, are in Me and I in You, that they also may be in Us, so that the world may believe that You sent Me.

—John 17:17,21

Of course, Light and truth are one and the same. Yeshua is the Way, the truth and the Life.

Yeshua said to him, *"I am the way, and the truth, and the life; no one comes to the Father but through Me.*

—John 14:6

He is also the Light of the World! So walking in the Light is walking in the truth, is walking in the Life of Yah (God)!

"I am the Light of the world; he who follows Me will not walk in the darkness, but will have the Light of life."

—John 8:12

Rabbi and I started singing this little tune, "Walking in the Light of Yah (God)" for quite a while doing intercession for all our loved ones, our families, spiritual children and for all of those that are connected with us in the ministry. It was wonderful!

Time literally "flew!" as we were declaring so and so "Walking in the Light of Yah!" There was great joy! And then an "earth-shaking," "life-transforming" revelation "hit me!"

The Speed of Light!

You see, the speed of light as researched by scientists is that one day=1,000 years! In other words: If you leave for space and you fly at the speed of light or almost at the speed of light, and you spend 1 day going and 1 day coming back on your space ship, you will be 2 days older, but those left behind on earth will be

2,000 years older! It is amazing that the Bible speaks about it even before science found this out!

The Word of Elohim says that to Him, one day is like 1,000 years! When we walk in the Light, the speed of light advances everything rapidly; breakthroughs come rapidly, setbacks, tests and painful circumstances disappear rapidly when we walk in the Light. In fact, all-natural substance and matter *disappear* when thrust into the speed of light! That is why Enoch "Walked with Elohim and was no more" because He was walking in the *Light* completely! So, he disappeared into the Light, Elohim took him!

Enoch walked with God; and he was not, for God took him.
—Genesis 5:24

In the same way, adverse natural circumstances that seem so threatening simply *disappear* when we walk in the Light.

Begin to declare it in your life: "I am walking in the Light of Yah," "I am talking, eating, working, flying, sowing, etc., in the Light of Yah!"

The power of death and life is in the tongue. Use your tongue to declare this powerful truth over your life and the life of your loved ones, and you will see great breakthroughs! The Angels are doers of the Word, they will do the words that you proclaim when they line up with Yah's words!

Bless YHVH, you His angels, Mighty in strength, who perform His Word, obeying the voice of His Word.
—*Psalms* 103:20

The 1,000 Fold Anointing!

But do not let this one fact escape your notice, beloved, that with the LORD one day is like a thousand years, and a thousand years like one day.

—2 Peter 3:8

As I was meditating on this powerful truth, the revelation "hit me!" This is the 1,000 fold anointing! One day is like one thousand years to ADONAI; that is the speed of light! You see, every time that we have received offerings, we pray the 1,000 fold anointing on it! This revelation came to Rabbi Baruch, who received it from David Herzog when this powerful evangelist and friend was preaching. David said that if we sow into the glory (when a preacher is preaching and the anointing is flowing, it is called "sowing into the glory" based on Galatians 6:6-8), we can reap 1,000 fold!

Rabbi Baruch ran to give David his last 50 shekels, and within 24 hours, he received a Mitsubishi van from a couple of believers in Jerusalem that was worth 50.000 shekels! Since then, he started to pray the 1,000 fold anointing of multiplication!

This is called Reaping in the Light of Yah (God), reaping at the speed of light! One day is like 1,000 years to ADONAI! You see, that is a multiplication of 365,000! It is when a natural seed (money or any other material asset!) loses its "materiality" and becomes light! At the speed of light, it disappears; it changes into light! Then that natural seed becomes *glorious,* and the reaping is *supernatural,* not only in supernatural 1,000 fold finances but in healing, deliverance, salvation, favor, breakthrough, joy, shalom and *no limitations*!

1,000 Fold Increase Is a Covenant Promise!

May YHVH, the Elohim of your fathers, increase you a thousand-fold more than you are and bless you, just as He has promised you!

—Deuteronomy 1:11

The least one shall become a thousand [a clan], and the small one a strong nation. I, the LORD, will hasten it in its [appointed] time.

—Isaiah 60:22 AMP

SOW TO THE SPIRIT, REAP 1,000 FOLD!

Even though the creational law of sowing and reaping says: Whatever you sow, you reap. If you sow tomatoes, you reap tomatoes. The supernatural law of sowing and reaping goes much higher!

For he who sows to his own flesh (lower nature, sensuality) will from the flesh reap decay and ruin and destruction, but he who sows to the Spirit will from the Spirit reap eternal life.

—Galatians 6:6-8

Sowing to the Spirit is not a "natural" thing to do! If the Spirit is the "soil" of your financial seed to those who teach you the Word and are anointed, then the multiplication of the seed is at the speed of light, which is the realm of the Spirit, the realm of the glory! That is why when we sow monetarily to those that preach, teach and minister the Word to us, our reaping is at the speed of light. We do not only reap money (because we sowed money; we reap *Eternal Life*! Eternal Life is the realm of Yah's glory, and in the glory, there is no lack, no sickness, no sin, no depression, no limitations! So we reap 1,000 fold prosperity, 1,000 fold healing and wholeness, 1,000 fold life!

Sow to the Spirit and reap Abundant/Eternal Life at the speed of light! Now, that is an earth-shaking revelation!

We Defy the World's Financial System When We Sow Right!

"There is a lad here who has five barley loaves and two fish, but what are these for so many people?"

—John 6:9

Yeshua operated in the 1,000 Fold Anointing when He multiplied the seed sown by a little child that had a spirit of generosity and donated all the food that he had to the ministry of Yeshua. We need to understand that this child came prepared to give and to bless. He certainly could not have eaten two fish and five loaves by himself! According to the Torah, it is very clear that the disciples need to bless the rabbi that teaches them materially. Most probably, when his mom packed his lunch for the journey, she packed more than enough for the child to bless Rabbi Yeshua and His 12 Ministers—Apostles! She knew that we should never come to any spiritual meeting, to the presence of ADONAI, empty-handed!

And none shall appear before Me empty-handed.

—Exodus 23:16

The Master took the two fish and the five loaves, blessed them and fed about 2,0000 people (5000 men + women and children!). On top of it, He had 12 baskets full of leftovers. The leftovers were the: *Harvest* at the speed of light of that little child! He went home probably to feed his entire village in the Galilee with 12 baskets full!

When they were filled, He said to His disciples, "Gather up the leftover fragments so that nothing will be lost."

—John 6:12

Walk in the Light of Yah (truth, holiness and Righteousness), Give and sow in the Light of Yah (with a pure heart and not from selfish ambition!) and *reap at the speed of light* much more than finances, healing, deliverance, salvation...

Declare the Word (I am walking, living, sowing, giving, etc., in the Light of Yah!) and that seed will not return empty; sow into the Spirit as you give to your teachers and you will reap everlasting, abundant life at the speed of *light*! Stay in faith with this because faith is the realm of Yah's *Light*; that is where the true speed of light happens! Unbelief is ignorance and darkness. True faith is *light*!

And without faith it is impossible to please Him, for he who comes to God must believe that He is and that He is a rewarder of those who seek Him.

—Hebrews 11:6

When we apply these principles and obey His Commandments during the times of financial shakings, we will rise to the top at the speed of light!

YHVH will make you the head and not the tail, and you only will be above, and you will not be underneath, if you listen to the commandments of the YHVH your God, which I charge you today, to observe them carefully.

—Deuteronomy 28:13

Sowing into the spirit is a commandment; reaping 1,000 fold at the speed of light is the result of obedience!

Appendix
More Books

Order now online: www.kad-esh.org/shop/

The MAP Revolution (Free E-Book)
Find Out Why Revival Does Not Come... Yet!

The Identity Theft
The Return of the 1st Century Messiah

From Sickology to a Healthy Logic
The Product of 18 Years Walking
Through Psychiatric Hospitals

ATG: Addicts Turning to God
The Biblical Way to Handle Addicts and Addictions

The Healing Power of the Roots
It's a Matter of Life or Death!

Grafted In
It's Time to Take the Nation's!

Sheep Nations
It's Time to Take the Nations!

Restoring the Glory: The Original Way
The Ancient Paths Rediscovered

Stormy Weather
Judgment Has Already Begun,
Revival is Knocking at the Door

Yeshua is the Name
The Important Restoration of the Original
Hebrew Name of the Messiah

The Bible Cure for Africa and the Nations
The Key to the Restoration of All Africa

The Key of Abraham
The Blessing or the Curse?

Yes!
The Dramatic Salvation of
Archbishop Dr. Dominiquae Bierman

Eradicating the Cancer of Religion
Hint: All People Have It

Restoration of Holy Giving
Releasing the True 1,000 Fold Blessing

Vision Negev
The Awesome Restoration of the Sephardic Jews

The Woman Factor by Rabbi Baruch Bierman
Freedom From Womanphobia

The Revival of the Third Day (Free E-Book)
The Return to Yeshua the Jewish Messiah

Music Albums
www.kad-esh.org/shop/

The Key of Abraham

Abba Shebashamayim

Uru

Retorno

Get Equipped & Partner with Us

Global Revival MAP (GRM) Israeli Bible School
Take the most comprehensive video Bible school online that
focuses on dismantling replacement theology.
For more information or to order, please contact us:

www.grmbibleschool.com

grm@dominiquaebierman.com

United Nations for Israel Movement
We invite you to join us as a member and partner with $25 a
month, which supports the advancing of this End time vision
that will bring true unity to the body of the Messiah. We will
see the One New Man form, witness the restoration of Israel,
and take part in the birthing of SHEEP NATIONS. Today is an
exciting time to be serving Him!

www.unitednationsforisrael.org

info@unitednationsforisrael.org

Global Re-Education Initiative (GRI)
Against Anti-Semitism

Discover the Jewishness of Jesus and defeat Christian anti-Semitism with this online video course to see revival in your nation!

www.against-antisemitism.com

info@against-antisemitism.com

Join Our Annual Israel Tours

Travel through the Holy Land and watch the Hebrew Holy Scriptures come alive.

www.kad-esh.org/tours-and-events/

To Send Offerings to Support our Work

Your help keeps this mission of restoration going far and wide.

www.kad-esh.org/donations

CONTACT US

Archbishop Dr. Dominiquae & Rabbi Baruch Bierman

Kad-Esh MAP Ministries | www.kad-esh.org

info@kad-esh.org

United Nations for Israel | www.unitednationsforisrael.org

info@unitednationsforisrael.org

Zion's Gospel Press | shalom@zionsgospel.com

52 Tuscan Way, Ste 202-412, 32092 St. Augustine Florida, USA
+1-972-301-7087

CPSIA information can be obtained
at www.ICGtesting.com
Printed in the USA
LVHW042256040123
736509LV00005B/378